# Tim in Sand

by Tristan Horrom
illustrated by Eva Vagreti

Decodable 4



McGraw Hill Education

Bothell, WA • Chicago, IL • Columbus, OH • New York, NY

**MHEonline.com**



Send all inquiries to:
McGraw-Hill Education
8787 Orion Place
Columbus, OH 43240

ISBN: 978-0-02-133271-7
MHID: 0-02-133271-1

Printed in the United States of America.

7 8 9 LCR 25 24 23

It is Tim.

It is sand.

Tim hits sand.

Tim sits.

Is Tim in sand?

Tim sits in sand!